All Scripture references taken from the KJV of the Holy Bible, unless otherwise indicated.

The Battlefield of Marriage

by Dr. Marlene Miles

Freshwater Press 2023

ISBN: 978-1-963164-04-6

Paperback Version

Copyright 2023, Dr. Marlene Miles

All rights reserved. No part of this book may be reproduced, distributed, or transmitted by any means or in any means including photocopying, recording or other electronic or mechanical methods without prior written permission of the publisher except in the case of brief publications or critical reviews.

Table of Contents

Introduction 5
Prayer 7
They Want the Women 8
Already Defeated 17
Not Marriage Material 20
Captives 25
Spirit Spouse, Of Course 29
Man & Wife 34
It Takes a Lifetime 36
A Single Piece of Bread 38
Favor of the Lord 41
Thinking Like the Devil 44
The Defiling 47
Celebrity Spirit Spouse? 52
Men *or* Women 55
Disgrace the Enemy 56
To Disgrace the Church 59
The Defiler 62
These Are Not War Games 65
Married Off 67
Anti-Marriage Forces 69

Sliding Into DM's	74
Spilled Seed	76
Air Force	80
Wild Oats	83
Pray	87
Dear Reader	95
Other books by this author	96

The Battlefield of Marriage

Introduction

> When men began to multiply on the face of the land and daughters were born to them, the sons of God saw that the daughters of men were attractive, and they took as their wives any they chose (Genesis 6)

The above verse sets the backdrop for why marriage is a battlefield; *sons* of God covet the daughters of men and marry them. Sons of God in that verse are fallen angels. The verse says they took as wives as they chose. How is this possible? This book will explain it.

When you think of marriage being a battlefield you may think I mean *in* the marriage. No, it shouldn't be a battle *in* the marriage--, but sometimes it is.

The first marital battle for any person is to meet your kingdom spouse. There are other battles after that, including:

- Get married,
- Stay married, and
- Be happy in marriage.

Those things are not impossible; as a matter of fact, it is God's plan for us.

Prayer

Father, thank You for this word today. May it provoke thought, may it be very provoking to change, and may it bring deliverance to the hearers and the new understanding to their lives and what is right for them based on what you will have us to do, not just what we want to do in the Name of Jesus.

Amen

They Want the Women

> When man began to multiply on the face of the land and daughters were born to them, the sons of God saw that the daughters of men were attractive and they took as their wives any they chose,
> (Genesis 6)

Men, don't give up, but the daughters of men are in very high demand. If every man competing for the woman you want has more money than you, you may lose heart. If all the men competing for your beloved are better looking than you, if they have better personalities, more smarts – every possible attribute surpassing you, you might lose heart, you might give up. Don't give up.

What if the *man* that competes against you for the love of your life plays every dirty trick in the book, and plays tricks that are not even *in* the book? What if you didn't read the book, or didn't know there was a *book*?

What if this romantic competitor is invisible, so you don't even see him do it? He's invisible, so you don't even know anyone did anything at all, or that anything was done.

If you are not spiritual, you will not believe that to get married is a battle, or that there is an opponent at all. If you are not spiritual you will not believe that there is anything at all in the spirit or happening in the spirit, least of all invisible forces that have the ability or the interest to act against you.

Instead, when something negative happens in your interpersonal relationship, you may become jealous, looking at your human buddies, or every stranger, wondering if they want your lady. Maybe they do, maybe they don't. Your real competition is in the spirit, and it is the fallen angels, called sons of God in Genesis 6:6.

Now, don't lose interest thinking that no woman you want wants you, or you may think all that's left are women you aren't interested in when all the while the situation has been manipulated, and the *women* may have been manipulated.

Women may or may not know that they have been manipulated, or that the dating/marriage dynamic has been tampered with, and for generations, since Genesis.

One of the enemy's tricks is to pit men and women against one another. He's been doing that since Adam said that there was something wrong with the woman that God gave him. Was there anything wrong with Eve BEFORE

Adam sinned? Then how is Eve a problem now, but Adam doesn't admit that **he** has changed, or that *he* is now *defective*? My Bible does not show Adam or Eve apologizing or repenting, or renouncing the sin, to God. The unrepentant either believe they are not responsible or accountable and will gladly let whoever is listening know who is to blame.

On Earth, among humans, marriage is a battle. The landscape on this Earth as it pertains to marriage is a battlefield. There's warfare involved in getting a Kingdom mate, warfare involved in marrying them. Warfare continues in the birthing of and raising righteous seed. And, more warfare in being happy in marriage and staying married.

There's warfare in staying married because there are marriage-failure forces coming against people in general, but especially Christians.

If you had any idea of how much warfare is involved, you would never take marriage for granted, not even for a moment. Meeting the right one is by divine appointment. If you are in God's purposes, you are fine. If the devil has jumped you into his timeline, then your divine partner may be ever elusive.

Being in the right location for you to find a spouse--, no, **your** spouse, may require warfare. You must know that the place where you are is a place that you are approved to be in. There are some places where you can't get a spouse, because you're not allowed to be in that land, or that territory—, to work in that land or to live there--, spiritually speaking.

As in the Bible, there are some places where you should not get a spouse. Abraham told his servants where to go to get a wife for Isaac and where not to go. Isaac and Rebekkah were grieved that Esau married a Canaanite woman (Genesis 26:35). Samson's parents had picked out a wife for him, but Samson wanted another woman that the parents didn't approve of: Delilah.

What and where are those places that you should not go, live, or seek a mate? It varies, God will have to tell you in your particular case.

This may sound like prejudice or intolerance, but it's Bible and I'd rather do it God's way than to fail or be miserable in disobedience.

If you are living in a wrong place and don't ask God about it, it is not likely that anyone is coming to make you move or go someplace else. But spiritually speaking, have you ever lived in a place where nothing worked? I don't mean in the house, but you lived in an area, a town, a neighborhood, and it just wasn't right for you?

You weren't supposed to be there. There are territorial demons, territorial powers over every region, state, and country. If things weren't working for you in a certain place, territorial powers were saying, *"No, no,* and no. If you are not saved, with the power of God working for you, then you're subject to the *No's* of those territorial powers.

When some territorial *spirit* is vetoing God's blessings, yes's and promises for you--, this means war. War means spiritual warfare.

If you are saved and you have the power of God, the Holy Ghost, and you know how to pray and engage in warfare, then you can overcome those things. But there will still be a battle. Depending on who you are to God and what your prayer life is like, *that is,* what your prayer altar is like, you can overcome those powers. If God sent you and you are supposed to be there, then you MUST overcome those territorial *spirits*.

The town adjoining the place I grew up in was one such place for the young men of that area. Once the sun went down, if any males from my hometown were found in that other town, they would be run out of that county, and sent back home. That is the physical following the spiritual; the boys from Town A were not allowed to date or marry the girls from Town B, says the people of Town B. Where would they get such an idea? Tradition. Culture. From the territorial spirits who just *put the idea in their minds*.

People of God, ideas come from the spirit world, all day and all night.

One fellow from Town A defied the directive not to marry a young lady from Town B; they eloped. The marriage was rocky, and they divorced when their children were very young. It was tough on all involved.

So if things are working well in your life, except your love life, suspect anti-marital forces may be working against you, either through your bloodline, if you see a pattern in your family. If you're the only one, then it's you. Don't just call yourself unlucky in love and give up; that's what the devil wants you to do. Warfare is required; fight for your marriage, your spouse, your children and family. Fight for your purpose and destiny.

You can win these battles!

My book, **What Do You Have to Declare?** is about territorial *spirits*.

Already Defeated

Have you noticed how many young people who say they don't want to get married? They don't even want to think about it. Unless they don't change their minds, and obey God, they are already defeated. They have already been defeated on the marriage battlefield, some without knowing they were even in a battle.

Just because you say you don't want to get married; it doesn't make you clever. You're not wiser than the next guy, you're less wise. You've already allowed the devil to take away one of the main **purposes** for being born on Earth, to get married and have a family and bringing forth righteous seed.

Be Fruitful & Multiply.

God said, **Be fruitful and multiply.** Humans multiply by sex. Sex consummates marriage. *Goes into* equals married in the Bible. In the entire Bible, and I haven't found any of the words that those who officiate read out of the tiny book they hold when performing weddings--, you know the *Dearly Beloved stuff.* Where is that from? My point is, if it is not in there, it wasn't used all throughout the Bible by those who got married. But those who got married in the Bible were married. Yes, Jesus went to a wedding feast in Canaan, so they did have weddings. But the couple **consummated** the marriage: *Goes into equals married.*

Following the laws of the land, of course, become legally married and then the consummation. After that, be fruitful and multiply because God wants more of you. God so loved the world, He not only gave His Son to die to save us all, He wants more of us--, more sons and daughters. Be fruitful and multiply.

Not Marriage Material

We skip ahead and let's say you've lived the life that you wanted to live, and you get to the Pearly Gates, and you are standing there to get in.

As the Church collectively, we are to be married to the Lamb of God, to be the Bride of Christ, individually, your concern is to get in.

So, you get to the Pearly Gates, but what if you can't get in? What if your entrance document has a stamp on it that says: **NOT MARRIAGE MATERIAL?** It may say that because you never got married, never wanted to get married and never tried to get married.

Or, you got married, but took nothing about it seriously. Do you realize that you made a vow before God and without fulfilling it, or at least trying to fulfill it, you did a worse thing than not making a vow at all? Vows to God are nothing to be toyed with. Marriage is a covenant, and it has **vows** with it.

Therefore, if you never get married, how will you ever know anything about being married to the Lamb of God? How will you ever know anything about being the Bride of Christ? How will you ever know anything about being married if you never get married? Don't make your decision to not marry be based on bad marriages you've seen, especially your parents', if that was the case.

Don't let the devil steal this away from you. If he has, you need to fight and get it back.

Ok--, we have just left the future time at the Pearly Gate--, now you're back on Earth living in the present.

The Word says we're supposed to work out our salvation with fear and trembling. So if you want to know that you're really saved, get married and **stay** married. It'll work out a lot in you.

Unsaved people can get married and stay married. Why can't <u>saved</u> people? Saved people: if you are saved and not perishing, you should honor God and get married, have a family and stay married.

But if you never get married, you might get to the Pearly Gates and have your application for entrance stamped: **NOT MARRIAGE MATERIAL.**

I pray that's not you.

If somebody has clearly laid out the rules for a thing, how do you think you can just change it because you feel like it or you don't agree with it? If that someone is God, why would anyone think that they can change spiritual law, or not obey it, and still think they will get the same results that the people who follow the rules will get?

You won't.

And you can't just opt out of marriage, as if you're refusing to receive texts from your credit card company. It doesn't work like that.

You don't want to be at the Pearly Gates and hear Saint Peter, who *they* say will be there, saying, *Well, we don't know if he's marriage material or not; he **opted out**.*

Well, did you opt out of breathing the air that God provided? Did you opt out of eating the food that's grown on this planet, or drinking the water? Did you opt out of enjoying the land, the sunshine, the oceans, or the people in general? No, you opted *in*. You opted in to everything when you were born here, on that day, that hour, that minute, that second you got here, you opted *in*.

You can't just change the rules because they seem inconvenient to you.

Captives

The people who don't want to get married, their minds and souls, and their spirits are being manipulated; they are in captivity. Those people are already captured by the devil. When your mind is not thinking the way that God designed it to think, and you're thinking anti-Kingdom, anti-God, anti-marriage--, your mind has already been captured and you're thinking just like the devil.

Men need to be especially careful, because the devil hates women. I'm sure he started the gender wars--, boys versus the girls, or Men versus Women, bros v. h…s – NO! That's denigrating and not of God. Don't think like the devil. You should be honoring women. You should appreciate women. You are to respect and protect women. Competing with or being against womenkind is not what God created man for.

We get thoughts sent to us all day, all of us, all day long, all night. We pick and choose among the thoughts and the influences and the impulses that come to us. And if we're in God, we pick the right ones and then act on those thoughts.

But if we are in our flesh, well, that's another whole thing.

Worse, when a soul is captive, it can't--, it just *can't*. It can't make Godly choices. It can't do Godly things. It can't do right because it has to do what the captor wants him to do. It's as though the person is under remote control or is brainwashed. The person controlled may or may not know that they are being controlled. They may argue with you that they are not, that they are their own man.

The suggestive and controlling rhetoric that comes to you either suddenly or slowly, gets into your head and you end up doing things that you may not have planned to do even things you swore in your life, you'd never do. Oh, saints of God, the devil can be subtle and tricky.

Right now, you may be thinking, *I'm not hearing any voices or thoughts.* Maybe you're not. Maybe you just get feelings--, sometimes you just *feel* like you don't want to do a thing or *feel* like you do want to do something.

Possibly you get mischievous ideas that you think are your ideas. They may not be your idea at all. Then the tricky devil may send a person in your life to help you not do what you're supposed to by distraction. Or, he may send someone to entice you to do the very thing you swore you'd never do. Well, the idea is already put in your head before the invitation in the natural presents. That's the devil.

Here's one that you hear on a lot of movies and TV shows too. How can you marry and just be with that one person for the rest of your life?

A person who had never thought that before in their life is now demonized to think like that. It's repeated over and again. It has become a mockery and laughed at publicly by many. In believing this, a man has to make other negative judgments against women, marriage, and ultimately the plan of God. But does he (or she) realize that they've done this? Maybe not, they just think they made an isolated decision to not marry, or to stay single. And, they believe they decided that independently.

Wow.

Spirit Spouse, Of Course

First of all, any of us should be glad that any one person would be able to stand us for the rest of our lives (Kat Williams). But pre-planning to weary of your spouse, or planning to need *different* is still devil talk. These thoughts are sponsored by the devil, most often, his representative, spirit spouse.

Spirit spouse jumps into a life as soon as it can. It is waiting for a human to get to Earth, if *spirit spouse* is embedded in your foundation and comes down your bloodline. It doesn't matter where it comes from. Once it gets to a human, it wants to stay. It is a demon.

It's been waiting for you, perhaps, and it's waiting also for your child and your grandchildren. When it gets into one family member, if not cast out, it lives in and tortures that bloodline, for generations. It is only there to steal, kill, and destroy.

Whether it comes in by ancestry, down foundational lines, or you invite it yourself by your own sin, when it arrives it wants to stay. You invite it in and you can keep it here by worshipping it. You worship spirit spouse by **sin**, usually sexual sin: fornication, adultery, masturbation, bestiality, and any other sexual perversions. The devil loves perversion.

Once it's allowed in, it gets attached. It thinks it marries you. Now it's in your soul. And now what you think is self-talk; is not. These thoughts you're getting, these impulses you're getting, is not self-talk at all, it's demon talk. It's the enemy talking to you. You think these are your own thoughts. They're not; it's spirit spouse. Its goal is to keep you from getting married in the natural world. You can date around all you like, but the minute you start to get serious toward someone, or someone starts getting serious about you, the spiritual war begins or heightens. Its goal is to keep you from having the possibility of righteous seed coming to this Earth. These demons try to block God, by blocking you.

It whispers things into your soul such as, *"She's not good enough for you. She's not pretty enough—hot enough. She's a gold digger. She's too thin, she's too heavy. You can do better. Don't you know you're a chick magnet? She doesn't even listen when you are talking to her."*

It says things such as, *"Men are all liars. You can't trust him. He's broke, you need a guy with more money. He doesn't even have a nice car or house. Look at how he dresses; he has no style. You can do so much better than him. He doesn't even listen when you are talking to him."*

These thoughts (words) are insidious and spirit spouse will have you thinking that <u>you</u> are "spiritual" and you just *discerned* all that. Spirit spouse will have you dismiss even good suitors or will cause them to run away from you for reasons unknown to you. Spirit spouse is especially on guard against you meeting, dating and marrying your kingdom spouse.

So, if you really think that this is God telling you not to get married, why don't you, with permission of your doctor, go on a three day fast, and ask God. Just ask Him, so you are not deceived. Do this so you can get rid of evil voices in your head. Fast; some come out by prayer and fasting. Do this to live a victorious Christian life.

If God is telling you not to get married, then He is calling you to chastity, to celibacy. God doesn't tell people to not get married so they can play the field and run the streets.

> But if they cannot contain, let them marry: for it is better to marry than to burn, (1 Corinthians 7:9)

Man & Wife

God made Adam, and then God made a wife for Adam. According to the Law of First Mention, God establishes a pattern and an expectation. God set forth many Laws in Genesis, one being Adam + Eve. God made a wife for Adam. He said be fruitful and multiply. Humans cannot multiply without sex. Sex is a covenant and *goes into* equals married. Eve was Adam's wife.

God made Adam and then God made a wife for Adam. Adam named this woman Eve. **Adam never complained to God that God had only given him one woman.** He complained about some other stuff, but that was never a recorded complaint.

Quiet those voices, get deliverance if necessary. Learn the Word of God and abide by it by yielding to the Holy Spirit. That is how you too can be married to one woman for the rest of your life--, it is God's plan. When God establishes a plan and tells people to do it, He gives them anointing and Grace to carry it out. That is how a woman can be married to one man for the rest of her life, as well; it is God's plan for your life.

In eternity, the Church will be married to the Lamb of God. We will be the Bride of Christ. That is one marrying One.

It Takes a Lifetime

If you can't get married and stay married to one person, you end up scattering yourself all over the Earth from house to house and down to town, person to person, neighborhood to neighborhood. Doing that, you never really build anything, any really good thing for your life because it takes a lifetime to build a life. It takes stability.

A *life* cannot be built in a year. Say you spend a year with someone, but then you stop building that life and then you break up, and get with another person; that is polygamy.

Jumping from person to person is polygamy, and polygamy is not of God.

God made Adam; God made Eve. Man came up with having multiple women when the demons of greed and *lust* jumped in. That's when and where they got the idea to have concubines and handmaidens. Many may think polygamy is having more than one spouse at a time. It is that, but it is more than that. When you have sex with an individual you just *married* them.

So multiple girlfriends, or boyfriends, even if one at a time, is still polygamy if you had sex with them. Sex created a covenant between the two of you, an evil soul tie. It is the devil's copy of a Godly marriage. In a sexually promiscuous society, practically everyone is polygamous, but that does not make it right or good.

My book, **Too Many Wives: Wonder Why You Have Lady Problems?** this is explored in more depth.

A Single Piece of Bread

Demons, especially *lust* demons want a person to have relations with as many people as possible. Yet, they can never be satisfied, but they will drive a man to the streets, to promiscuity, to poverty, to a single piece of bread. I heard a *Playa* once say, *"Sex? Who wants it? You can find sex when you can't find bread to eat."* Seems like he was finally learning from his sin life.

Jumping from person to person is polygamy. Polygamy is not of God, and it brings forth a lot of evil.

Adam and Eve, not Adam and as many women as Adam could get with.

Those who are pursuing as many women as they can get with, or as many men, as evil is equal opportunity, that is demonically influenced. Genesis 6 says, they took of the women any as they chose. They might as well have said as many as they chose because it's polygamy and it's demonic because a spirit spouse is not monogamous. Spirit spouse will sleep with everyone in a family, every one in a bloodline--, and do we think it is relegated to one bloodline? It's more like any as they choose, as many as they choose; they get in wherever they can get in, wherever they can fit in.

What do I mean by a demon having relations with people? Mostly it happens in their sleep. Sex in the dream. Waking up aroused and there is no one there but you. Sleep paralysis. Bed going down but there is no one there. Repeated yeast or other infections, and you're not even having relations with anyone, in the natural. Eating in the dream; being fed in the dream. Dreams wiped. No, not all of these symptoms, any of these symptoms is a sign of spirit spouse. I am sure there are more.

Favor of the Lord

He who finds a wife, it says in Scripture, finds a good thing and obtains favor from the Lord. If we break that down, he who has no natural wife has no *good thing*, and does not get favor from the Lord. And to not have a Lord's favor is living at extreme disadvantage, if it's living at all.

The favor of the Lord lasts a lifetime. The favor of the Lord is life. Psalm 30.

For you, o Lord, will bless the righteous with favor. You surround him as with a shield, (Psalm 5:12).

Favor is protection for your life. Jesus increased in wisdom and stature, and in favor with God and man. Luke 2: 52, so, of course it is totally desirable.

So, when you are not in favor with God, then you may have the disfavor of mankind. If you are not in favor with God, folks you meet may have reproach toward you for no apparent reason. You don't get blessings and perks that other people may be getting. You may be turned off or turned away, turned around and turned down because of the reproach. This is the opposite of being in God's favor.

Saints, it is natural to do the things that God instructed us to do unless we're in captivity, and/or brainwashed by the devil. It is natural to be attracted to someone and get all coupled up. That's natural. It is God's way, and it is also prophetic vision of Christ being married to the Church, even though married in this Earth, is a battlefield, we can still be victorious; we don't have to fall for the enemy's tricks.

The devil despises women. He has no use for them. That's because, God has given women authority to bruise the devil's head.

> And I will put enmity between thee and the woman, and between thy seed and her seed. It shall bruise thy head, and thou shalt bruise his heel, (Genesis 3:15).

We have authority to bruise the head of the enemy. Not only that, but our righteous seed also that we should be bringing to Earth with the help of a Kingdom spouse, shall bruise his head.

Thinking Like the Devil

We really weren't born thinking like the devil, were we? Some were born that way, and until they get delivered, they really are not marriage material. Please stop looking for bad boys or outrageous girls as potential Kingdom spouses. They can be spouses, but God is not sponsoring that.

Anyone who thinks like the devil but wasn't born that way, has been captured and is captive.

We need to pray the Lord to turn our captivity, to deliver us from our captors and from the enemy, in the Name of Jesus.

You may be thinking, *I'm not captive. I have control of my body; I'm walking around the Earth. I'm doing all kinds of things. I'm doing what I want.*

Yeah, but if your mind is tuned into the devil's channel. If you're programmed to do evil instead of good, you are most likely captive. You are programmed by the voices in your soul. Those voices tell you to destroy rather than to do good. If you obey those voices your programming hinders, interrupts, redirects, derails and/or destroys your own life, as well as the lives of others. This also brings trauma to their lives as well as your own.

A controlled captive rather than doing good and building up others, they tear others down. When you build up others, you also build the Kingdom, and you build yourself as well. When you tear down, it is the opposite, you work against the Kingdom of God and eventually everything you have done against someone else will backfire on you and come down on your own head. The pit dug for another will be inhabited by the digger – sooner or later.

It takes a lifetime to build a life.

The Defiling

Anyone who has read the Bible, including the devil knows that the Church is to be the Bride of Christ, so his strategy is to pollute and defile that Bride anyway that he can.

I'm not just talking about women; the devil doesn't care; he'll defile anybody if he can--, any gender.

> But when man began to multiply on the face of the land, and daughters were born to them, the sons of God saw that the daughters of man were attractive. And they took as their wives any they chose,
> (Genesis 6)

Men, how many wives can you choose because you want to? In our culture, one. In some other cultures, maybe more than one. But in the spirit--, how many? As many as you choose if you are a spirit spouse, you could keep choosing them because they don't know about each other if nobody's talking about it. If they also don't know that they've been taken as a wife, because they don't know the signs of being a captive bride, a captive wife, a captive spouse in the spirit then they won't even know that they *are one*.

Spirit spouse is not monogamous; they go for as many as they can. It is polygamous. It would like to marry ALL the women of its territory. It'll sleep with everyone in a family, and that's gross enough. It'll sleep with everyone down the bloodline. It's a demon, and you can't let it tell you how to think. And even though spirit spouse's ideas at the beginning seem as though they are benefiting your flesh, they are not. It is not a quiet, secret way to have your *needs* met and it's not hurting anything. It should not be kept a secret; you need deliverance. It is not *not* hurting anything or anyone; it will do tremendous damage as spirit spouse has nefarious plans.

They are supposed to look as though they are helping you in some way. That's the hook; it won't always be that way. As soon as it's fully embedded into your life, it's true colors will show because it comes to steal, kill, and destroy.

This is all complicated. Spirit spouse steals from people. It steals money. It steals time. It steals beauty, and youth. If steals virtues. It kills and destroys relationships. It demands sacrifice. And if you keep servicing it or serving it, that means you worship it. Worshiping gives it permission to take whatever it wants from you, whether you know what that something is or not, or that is going to be taken, or *when* it'll be taken.

People of God, there are astral projecting *spirit spouses* that are **not** sons of God. They are **human spirits** who have learned to do evil and get their powers from the devil. What they do is rape; it cannot be described another way. They are pure evil and are also are not monogamous, there is no reason why they should be. Many probably have a real wife and real kids at home.

In reality, your entire life stolen from you, it's no longer yours. And you think, as a man, you're running, running from women who want to marry you? Well, you're already married. You're already married to spirit spouse. How are you going to marry somebody else? You will have to get unmarried to spirit spouse first before really anybody wants you, in some cases before some people can even *see* you.

That goes for men and women. Did you used to get a lot of attention from the opposite gender and now it is as though you're invisible?

All of that is the work of spirit spouse.

So, you're trying not to get married when you're already married? You don't even know how many spirit spouses you may have. You may be married up to--, I don't know--, 30 or more times. There are more than thirty kinds of spirit spouses.

Spirit spouse is doing nothing for you; it doesn't care about you, or humans. It will kill and destroy. It'll wreck a relationship. It'll wreck a marriage. It'll wreck an engagement. It'll wreck a wedding. It'll wreck anything. It doesn't care. It is dangerous. It's jealous, covetous, hateful, and wicked.

Celebrity Spirit Spouse?

Spirit spouse is not just about looks. Anybody could have a spirit spouse. If it depended on looks, only supermodels would have them, but anybody can unfortunately have one, *or more*. It may come to you disguised as a human, but it is a demon, so trust that it doesn't care what *you* look like, it's not pretty. But that you are human, have human parts, and especially if you are a child of God; you are desirable to it.

Nowadays, if you listen to some celebrity interviews, you'll hear these various celebrities talking about sleeping with demons or spirits, things that come to them at night. They think it's cool, they think it's OK and they either don't know anything about this, they don't know what to call it, so they accept it. They may think it's just a dream. Remember, it can be very pleasing to the flesh--, at first.

Maybe these celebrities are all bought and paid for, so they have to say what is scripted for them to say in the natural, or they have to say what they've agreed to in the spirit, in the sleep, in the dream, or maybe in the *coven*. Maybe they do know better, but if an evil covenant has been made, without Jesus, they may feel that they have to abide by that covenant. Celebrities get used especially when they use their platforms of fame to spout demonic propaganda, mistruths, and lies. So much damage is done in the Earth by deceived or bought and paid for "celebrities."

Some of the signs of spirit spouse are: sex in the dream, the bed going down and there's no one there. Sleep paralysis, Getting married in the dream. Somebody handing you babies in the dream. Seeing babies in the dream. Feeding babies in the dream. Shopping in the dream. And dreams totally wiped. These are all signs of spirit spouse.

Obviously, some are signs of spirit children. Where there is a spirit spouse, there are spirit children. And when there are spirit children, spirit spouse will be so hard to dislodge until the spirit children are gone.

Oh, Blood of Jesus.

Lord, let the Holy Spirit purge out every evil marital magnet in my soul that has been designed by the enemy to ruin my marriage or to even take the desire to get married from me, in the Name of Jesus.

Lord, reverse our captivity in the Name of Jesus. Amen.

Men *or* Women

So, these demons prefer women, but they'll get with men for a number of reasons. One is to keep the men from getting with women. And it's to defile the man. And it's to block righteous seed, and it's to pervert the use of man and then go and accuse that man or woman before God.

Genesis Six was a nice way of putting what the demons are doing with the daughters and some of the sons of men.

Disgrace the Enemy

In the Old Testament, in war, sleeping with the enemy's wife meant, you had disgraced your enemy, you had conquered your enemy, and you had defeated them utterly to the utmost.

In Genesis 35:22, regarding Reuben, it says:

> It came to pass while Israel dwelt in that land, that Reuben went and lay with Bilhah, his father's concubine, and Israel heard of it. And as a result of this adultery, he lost the respect of his father.

In addition to that, this happened to Bilhah, she had to live out the rest of her days as a widow. She still lives in the house, but she is basically put out to pasture because her husband will no longer want her after she sleeps with someone who is not her husband, and he finds out about it.

Reuben slept with his brother's mother. How gross and ungodly is this?

Absalom, on the advice of Ahithophel and Hushai did similarly.

Absalom said to Ahithophel, "Give us your advice. What should we do?"

Ahithophel answered, "Sleep with your father's concubines whom he left to take care of the palace. Then all Israel will hear that you have made yourself obnoxious to your father, and the hands of everyone with you will be more resolute." So they pitched a tent for Absalom on the roof, and he slept with his father's concubines in the sight of all Israel.

Now in those days the advice Ahithophel gave was like that of one who inquires of God. That was how both David and Absalom regarded all of Ahithophel's advice. (2 Samuel 16:17-23)

Absalom, David's son did the same thing, slept with King David's concubines. By so doing, both of those boys were sending messages to their dad. *I don't like you. I hate you. I'm conquering you. I'm defeating you. I'm sleeping with your woman or your women.*

To Disgrace the Church

So, when Spirit Spouse comes along to sleep with the Church. Capital letter church to sleep with the members of the Saints of God. It is saying that it is trying to conquer God. It is an antichrist, anti-marriage anti-Kingdom *spirit*, and it is saying I am sleeping with these women. We have conquered them whether they know it or not.

We have conquered them, and therefore we have conquered you. That is the message they're trying to send to God.

Spirit spouse is evil. It must be cast out of your life.

Three days later, while all of them were still in pain, two of Jacob's sons, Simeon and Levi, Dinah's brothers, took their swords and attacked the unsuspecting city, killing every male. They put Hamor and his son Shechem to the sword and took Dinah from Shechem's house and left. The sons of Jacob came upon the dead bodies and looted the city where their sister had been defiled. They seized their flocks and herds and donkeys and everything else of theirs in the city and out in the fields. **They carried off all their wealth and all their women and children, taking as plunder everything in the houses.**

Dinah in Genesis 35:38 went out to the land, and she was attacked. The brothers wanted vengeance against that whole city because their only sister had been carried off and raped by one man, the prince of that city.

Once Dinah's brothers and other avengers took over and looted the whole city, they carried off all the wealth of the city and all the women and the children.

They took the women--, which means, *I have defeated you, I have captured you.*

They defiled the women. Once a woman is defiled, the man usually doesn't want her again, or to have children with her (Old Testament).

In the spirit, defiling is foul, and it is serious. Whether a person can see in the spirit or not, this defiling is real. It puts a wrong garment on that woman. A soiled, filthy garment is put on her in the spirit, and her glory is taken. Her star is taken, or it's covered, exchanged or stolen, and her beauty is covered as by a covering cast or an evil veil.

Her intended, whoever her real Kingdom spouse is supposed to be may not even be able to *see* her.

The Defiler

This is what the battlefield of marriage on Earth looks like. We all should be on a quest to get married to our Kingdom spouse.

Please know that this is a spiritual endeavor. You can gain weight, lose weight, change your hair and your clothes all you want, but unless you fight spiritual defilement in the spirit, there is nothing in the physical you can do to override this. You can try all kinds of worldly lotions, potions, and concoctions--, nothing and no one but Jesus can fix this major spiritual problem.

Women of God, this is very serious. The same person who defiled you may be the very person who rejects you and that person MAY have been the one to be your husband. If he is as out of order as you are, then the devil could have jumped any *spirit* in him to defile you which allowed the devil to put that nasty garment and reproach on you, as well. We've seen it so many times, men who have disdain and no respect for women that they were head over heels in love with, until they had sex with her.

So close, but yet so far. This may be the cry of the woman who says, *"I was sure he was the one. I was so sure, and he was too, that we went ahead and had sex."* That could have been a divine connection, but if it does not proceed according to God's order and timing, what God meant for your good the devil could sabotage. By having sex prematurely, even with the RIGHT person, all kinds of demons could be introduced and invited into your relationship to destroy it.

Remember this from now on: RIGHT ONE at the RIGHT TIME, in God's right order.

Marriage is under attack. It always has been. Women are under attack; they've been since Genesis. Men should be protecting women, but some of them are not. Some are helping the devil, by attacking the women, leaving them exposed, unprotected, and traumatized, as Hamor did to Dinah.

These Are Not War Games

Whether you're a man or a woman, do you like video war games? There's really no time to be playing and no need to really be playing video war games when your real life is a warfare.

You could use some of that time and energy that you put into fake games, and video games, for strategy and apply it to your real life in spiritual warfare, in study and praise and prayer and worship, your life could be amazing.

While I do not disparage all video games or having some down time and entertainment, be sure you are exerting at least that much energy in building your life. You know the life that it takes a lifetime to build. Your marriage could be amazing. Your spouse could be amazing. Your children and your legacy could be amazing. Your *bloodline* could get a good report from God when it's all said and done and you're trying to get through the Pearly Gates.

Marriage is a battle. The landscape is a battlefield because of the warfare involved in meeting and marrying a Kingdom mate. There is warfare involved in having kingdom children and raising them up; they are righteous seed. And there's more warfare after that to stay married.

Married Off

The fact that it's so hard is a clue of how important it is and, how critical marriage is for your life, your destiny and your legacy. It is nothing to play with if you're supposed to be part of the Bride of Christ

The devil has created, 33 flavors of *spirit spouse*, and all of them want to marry you. The devil wants to get you married to some demon before you get a chance to marry Jesus.

The devil wants you to be defiled, and once you are you may start to miss divine connections.

The defiling occurs because if you sin, you fall out of God's divine plan for your life and fall into the devil's evil timeline. From there, satanic appointments are made for you. Haven't you ever thought or said, *"Why does the same stuff keep happening to me? Why do I keep meeting this same kind of guy/girl? There's got to be something else better out there."* That's because of evil foundation, and/or your own sin.

It will repeat until you repent.

But when you are in purpose and on Godly timelines, that should never happen, in the Name of Jesus. Being in purpose protects you from falling into the devil's clutches.

Still, none of us are perfect. We thank God for the atoning Blood of Jesus Christ. Amen.

Anti-Marriage Forces

This is not all spiritual stuff. There's warfare in the natural, too. The warfare that is created in the spirit will come to the natural, if it is not handled in the spirit. The battles fought in the natural are because of things not being handled in the spirit.

Let's say you're in a restaurant with your husband. Anti marriage forces are deployed to interfere and to get into your marriage no matter where you are, whether you're both together or not, day or night. And they are deployed to interfere with your relationships and to get all up in your business like they say.

This particular night they find you two having a meal in a restaurant. You notice someone trying to check out your person. They may not even want your person, but they see you and you've got the Spirit of God in you. They hate you, instantly. The *spirit* in them hates you immediately. Next, they size you up. Then they want to conquer you.

What is the strategy to conquer you? Sleep with your woman. Sleep with your wife. How do they plan to conquer you? Sleep with your husband. That says, *I've conquered you; I've defeated you.*

You're of God? They hate the Spirit of God in you. Perhaps they know that we have more authority and power over them. If you didn't know it before, you know it now. Amen.

The demons of random unsaved folks hate you; it's built in. There's enmity built right in. Saved people can have demons as well, demons hate the Spirit of God, no matter who they are in.

Now your person has been flirted with, or hit on. If your person, your man, for example, is a carnal person, and they're getting attention from strangers, things could go wrong. Accosted by a strange man, a strange woman--, this could go to their head. They may start to believe or be affirmed in what they've always wanted: to be super attractive to the opposite gender.

But this is way deeper than looks, swag, or sex-appeal. It's far more complicated than just that.

If this attention goes to their head, the *spirit of vanity* will come in. They may start telling their buddies about how women are always checking them out. Then the *spirit of lust* comes with *vanity;* they travel together.

Your person may not have been *pulling* at all. It was just that the anti-marriage person that came after them was on assignment to break up a marriage, your marriage in particular, or any marriage that they could possibly break up.

All this happened in the spirit before it got to the natural, long before any of you got to the restaurant that evening. That either of you were a candidate for this attack could have started at either of your spiritual foundations. Have you and your spouse addressed your individual foundation issues? *That* this anti-marriage attack has a footing could be related to some type of unrepented sin in either of you. What's your prayer life like, especially repentance? One spouse cannot leave it for the other spouse to do all the praying in a marriage. Don't you get up in the morning and shower yourself, *yourself*?

Or, is the praying spouse doing all the showering for the <u>couple</u>?

It makes no sense, so even if one of you is more spiritual and well versed in the things of God, the other doesn't just hang on like dead weight to receive the blessings. If one knows and pursues as much knowledge of God and the kingdom as they can, but the other knows nothing of God, what will the two talk about? How will they communicate? How can they agree?

Your Kingdom spouse will be likeminded; both of you should be God-focused.

Sliding Into DM's

If ani-marriage demons have knocked on the door of an egotistical person or a narcissist, and been invited in, the devil is ready to have a field day in that person's life and marriage.

Oh yeah, I look good. I know I look good. Everywhere I go, the ladies, the men are checking me out. They're sliding into my DM's. This new conceited way of thinking, for a formerly decent guy – compliments of spirit spouse.

Saints of god: Every opportunist and lustful predator in the world is sliding into as many DM's as they can; it is not just yours.

However, I don't want to offend anyone. You are gorgeous. You are handsome. You are *all that.* But all *that* belongs to your spouse, whether married yet or not, it belongs to your spouse prophetically. Whether you've met your person, your Kingdom spouse or not, it still belongs to your Kingdom spouse. It is not for the population at large.

Don't give it away.

It doesn't matter who you are with, or what they look like, somebody's gonna want them because <u>you're</u> with them, or *appear* to want them because they're with you.

Don't get me started on *greatly fearing* – if you greatly fear that someone wants your mate, you are assisting in drawing some of these anti-marriage, anti-kingdom people to him, or her.

As I said, it's very complicated.

Spilled Seed

Another thing God hates is spilled seed. The devil wants man to spill seed because God hates it. God killed Onan for spilled seed, killed him.

Spilled seed is one of the goals of the female *spirit spouse*, as she is on assignment to get seed from man. As said, it's pleasurable to the flesh for a while. It's pleasurable, until it is not--, until it is torture, until it is forced--, until it is rape. It is a pleasurable, dirty little secret until it separates you from friends, events, and society as it's desire is to sequester you to itself. Captive.

The devil is tricky; he has devised uses for human fluids. He has evil uses for human parts and organs, even while you still think you have the part--, it's complicated. More than one deliverance minister has books on deliverance of body parts. Google the subject; get your hands on that material.

If you don't know what *spirit children* are, ask God. Inquire from Him if you have any, and how many you have. If He doesn't tell you while you're walking around in the daytime, living your entertainment life, go to sleep. Go to sleep sober after asking Him, and you will have a dream. **God will show you if you ask Him how many *spirit children* you have. Ask if you have a spirit spouse, and ask how many.**

Know that there are no *spirit children* if there's no spirit spouse.

But what do you think the spilled--, I mean stolen *seed* is <u>for</u>?

A person could have more than one spirit spouse. The more important you are to God, and the more important you are to the plan of God, the more spiritual spouses you may have. You may have inherited one or more. You could have invited one or more by your own sin--, usually sexual sin. You could have been *sent* a spirit spouse by an evil human agent of the devil who hates you.

To torment you? Yes.

To steal from you? Yes.

To ruin your life. Uh huh.

To keep you from getting married in the natural? Uh-huh.

To get you into fights with your real spouse? Yup.

To get you divorced. Yes, for any of those reasons, and maybe others that are more heinous.

Humans, it is our job to know something about this, because marriage, getting married and staying married is a battlefield. But it's a war we're supposed to fight and win.

Some of those idols in evil foundations have claimed the sexual rights of the individual, which is to preclude them from marriage, being happy in marriage, and staying married. Sexual rights further attaches reproductive rights. Complicated, and sinister.

Having children can be part of this warfare. Take note of my books, **Barrenness** and **Fruit of the Womb (Barrenness 2)**. These books have warfare prayers that reach to the foundation to right the curse of barrenness in the believer's life. *Barrenness* is not just about children; it is about your successes and money as well.

Air Force

Exert your warfare energy on your real life and it could go very well for you. In prayer, decrees, and declarations, one person could put 1000 angels to flight. Two people, **in agreement**, could put 10,000 to flight. You like wars and war games? Well, these are warrior angels-- 1000 of them at your disposal.

Ten thousand angels will obey the voice of the Word of God out of your mouth when you have a Kingdom spouse and you two are in **agreement**. So, get married and master this Godly Air Force. Become a mighty force, in this Earth with your Kingdom spouse.

Men, stay with the wife of your youth; there is power, reward and favor in that. Do not be drawn away by foolish lusts. Drink from your own cistern all your life, so when it's all said and done, you will know what marriage is about, what it's like. It assists in the working out of your salvation with fear and trembling, but with help from the Heavens. Two is better than one because they have a good reward. Your salvation will have been worked out.

Know that a threefold cord is not easily broken. Be sure that the Holy Spirit is in your marriage; He is the third in a couple's union.

Your application through the Gates of Heaven when it's time, not before, can be stamped, **MARRIAGE MATERIAL.**

Man, you can't just leave it all for the woman to do. Pray together, study together, learn together. The man leads the home. It's the way God intended it. If the woman has her spiritual self together and the man doesn't, *who* is he going to lead?

Right now, I'm dealing with a 2-year dental assistant who is angry because they want to be the lead instead of a recently hired 14-year veteran assistant. The younger's rationale is that they were there first. No, they weren't. There is dental assisting, not the particular office, so the older assistant was Assisting first, learning and experiencing it; that one was **_there_** first.

Similarly, people of God, especially men, get your spiritual selves together so you can be in right position in the marriage, and in the home.

Wild Oats

Some say women are more sensitive to God. Well, the woman historically has been at home learning how to be a wife and a mother, staying out of trouble while the man has been out in the streets doing what he wants to do, picking up all kinds of ways, attitudes, and demons. He's been out there sowing *wild oats*. While he thinks he's having fun, just as many, or more *wild oats* have been sown into him, by wild demons and rioting *spirits*.

He's been *out there* having more experiences than she has. So many things are sexually transferred and sexually communicated.

The woman is not the same way, unless she's been out on the streets too--, chasing people, and receiving demons. Staying home does not exempt anyone from this; we are all born into a spiritual foundation and whatever is in there, is in there and transferable by contact, relationship, and blood.

Mostly women have been trained to be good girls and go to church; but that's not always the case.

Men are good; all of them are not bad. But the makeup of demons or idols, idol *gods* in anyone's soul determines how you think, or how you *think* you're thinking. It determines what thoughts are coming into your mind. When these devil-inspired thoughts fully grow up, in your understanding, in your head, in your heart, and then you act on them, your actions can create a myriad of problems in your life.

This is why some people have come to the decision that they don't want to get married, but it's not even their thought, and they don't even know it's not even their thought.

While you're on that three day fast, ask God about that. Ask Him about spirit spouses, and *spirit children.* Ask Him all of that. Then you need to get into some spiritual warfare.

Pray to get your foundation healed.

Pray that you'll get out of captivity.

Following is a short prayer, but look for a bigger prayer about marriage.

I recommend the ESM Prayer, how to get rid of spirit spouse on my channel. That prayer is based on the book, **Evil Spirit Marriage: Everyone Has A Spirit Spouse** by Pastor Dr.

Anthony O. Akerele; it is how I found that ministry, Mountain of Fire Virginia.

The purpose of spirit spouse in any believer's life is to mock God. Since God is not mocked, God will honor your request to banish spirit spouse from your life. Remember you do your part though, you have to confess, repent, and resist the devil--, all devils.

That's an important prayer, use it for your edification and your deliverance. Amen.

Pray

Lord, in the Name of Jesus, I ask that You hear my prayer today, and that You'll answer as You always do.

Thank You, Lord,

Answer with signs and wonders and deliverance and peace and joy.

Answer with victory and success, in the Name of Jesus. Lord, I repent of every sin that I've committed against You. Sins of omission, sins of Commission, since that I know that I committed that were hidden to me. Lord, forgive and have mercy upon me, in the Name of Jesus.

Lord, I repent for the sins of my parents and for my ancestors, all the way back to before Adam and Eve. There I retrieve my essence and my glory, in the Name of Jesus.

Lord, let all evil counsels against my getting married, and staying happily married collapse, in Jesus' Name.

Any ungodly, unethical, immoral association, with no divine purpose, between my spouse and any stranger, be scattered now, in the Name of Jesus.

Lord, remove all irrational fear that I may have that my spouse will be stolen from me, in the Name of Jesus.

Every demonic in-law, lose your hold upon my life, in Jesus' Name.

Every demonic ex and ex-in-law, lose your hold and take your word curses and evil wishes off my life; back to sender, in the Name of Jesus.

Spirit husbands and spirit wives, lose your hold on me, my life and that of my spouse, in the Name of Jesus.

Lord, if I am single, put my name on the Register of those who are available to be married.

Do not send any inappropriate suitors to me, in the NOJ. Block every unacceptable, inappropriate suitor that the enemy may send, in the Name of Jesus.

In the Name of Jesus, Lord, I reject every adversary. I reject every enemy; Lord, send me a likeminded soul mate, not a roommate, cell mate, or a jail mate, in the Name of Jesus.

Lord, send me a communicator, one who says what they mean, truth in love and one who hears me when I speak, so that we are mutually respectful of one another.

Lord, send me a suitor who wants to get married—someone likeminded, first having their mind on You and then on marriage, building, and fulfilling destiny, not someone I have to urge, or talk in to matrimony, in the Name of Jesus.

Strongmen at the gate of my marital breakthrough, be bound and removed by mighty warrior angels of God. Lift up ye heads oh ye gates of marital breakthrough, the King of Glory will come in. The LORD strong and mighty in battle, in Jesus' Name.

Any authority that stands in the way of my marriage, be defeated, in the Name of Jesus.

Let all property of the devil and evil traditions, strongholds of the mind, in my life that is obstructing my marriage receive Holy Ghost Fire, in the Nane of Jesus.

Lord, let every weapon used against my marriage backfire, in Jesus' Name.

Idols manipulating the message of Heaven in my mind, die to your roots, in the Name of Jesus.

Confusion as a weapon in my relationship, backfire, in the Name of Jesus.

I divorce and/or break every plan of the devil that he has planned for me, through spirit spouse or any other means, in the Name of Jesus.

Every astral projection assigned against me, die by Fire in Jesus' Name.

Any wicked power calling forth my spirit, you are a liar, die, in Jesus' Name.

Every familiar spirit assigned against me, DIE by Fire, in the Name of Jesus.

My spirt man, reject every witchcraft call, in the Name of Jesus.

Every power bewitching my star, fall down and die in Jesus' Name.

Lord, have mercy: do not let me suffer for things I knew nothing about in the past; I am in Christ now.

Lord Jesus, call my kingdom spouse to me, and me to my kingdom spouse today, in the Name of Jesus.

Lord, make Your perfect will for my marriage plain to me, in the Name of Jesus.

Lord bless me to do Your will and Your purpose now, and after marriage, in the Name of Jesus.

Lord, let me win this war of marriage, this battle to be fruitful and multiply in marriage, in the Name of Jesus.

Every curse that has been issued against my marriage is now cancelled, in the Name of Jesus.

Every demonic mark contrary to a settled home, be wiped off by the Blood of Jesus.

The spiritual marriage of my spouse to his or her parent, be dissolved, and let my spouse cleave to me as God ordained, in the Name of Jesus.

Anything that is blocking me from cleaving to my spouse, scatter, in the Name of Jesus.

Every inherited *spirit* that is not of God, go out of my life, out of my soul, in the Name of Jesus.

Any curse issued against my marriage or against my marital life, be broken, in the Name of Jesus.

Any power which says I will not enjoy marriage, be roasted by Holy Ghost Fire, in the Name of Jesus.

Any spirit that thinks it has married me or has control over my sexual rights, be destroyed by the power in the Blood of Jesus.

Any power that has taken my sexual rights, let my sexual rights go, NOW! And fall down and die, in the Name of Jesus.

Astral projecting spirit spouses, be captured in the spirit on the way to my house by mighty angels of God. You are not invited or welcome in my life. The Blood of Jesus is between me and you, in the Name of Jesus.

Spirit spouses of any source, origin, kind, or type, fall down and die, in the Name of Jesus.

Lord, thank You for Your Word, Your truth, Your peace, and for deliverance, in the mighty Name of Jesus.

I seal these declarations across every timeline, every dimension, every realm, past, present, and future, to Infinity, in the Name of Jesus.

I command that any attacks because of these prayers will backfire to sender seven times, in the Name of Jesus, *Amen*.

Dear Reader

Thank you, dear reader for acquiring and reading this volume. May it make a difference in your life. May your marriage be a Kingdom marriage, may it last and be happy and successful with kingdom children. Let your salvation be worked out and may your entrance into the Gates of Heaven at the appointed time, be glorious.

Until then, honor God every day of your life, in the Name of Jesus.

Amen.

Dr. Marlene Miles

Other books by this author

AK: The Adventures of the Agape Kid

AMONG SOME THIEVES

Ancestral Powers

Battlefield of Marriage (The)

Blindsided: *Has the Old Man Bewitched You?*

https://a.co/d/5O2fLLR

Churchzilla, The Wanna-Be, Supposed-to-be Bride of Christ

Demons Hate Questions

Devil Weapons: Unforgiveness, Bitterness,...

Dream Defilement

Don't Refuse Me, Lord (4 book series)

Every Evil Bird

Evil Touch

Fantasy Spirit Spouse

FAT Demons (The): *Breaking Demonic Curses*

The Fold (5 book series)

The Fold (Book 1)

Name Your Seed (Book 2)

The Poor Attitudes of Money (3)

Do Not Orphan Your Seed (4)

For the Sake of the Gospel (5)

Gates of Thanksgiving

got HEALING? Verses for Life

got LOVE? Verses for Life

got HOPE? Verses for Life

got money?

How to Dental Assist

How to Dental Assit2: Be Productive, Not Wasteful

Let Me Have A Dollar's Worth

Living for the NOW of God

Lose My Location
https://a.co/d/crD6mV9

Man Safari, *The* (mini book from Wilderness Romance)

Marriage Ed. Rules of Engagement & Marriage

Made Perfect in Love

Motherboard (The) - soul prosperity series

Plantation Souls

Power Money: Nine Times the Tithe

The Power of Wealth *(forthcoming)*

Rules of Engagement & Marriage

Seasons of Grief

Seasons of War

Sift You Like Wheat

Soul Prosperity soul prosperity series 3

https://a.co/d/5p8YvCN

Souls Captivity soul prosperity series 2

The Spirit of Poverty

This Is NOT That: How to Keep Demons from Coming At You

Throne of Grace: Courtroom Prayer

Time Is of the Essence

Too Many Wives: *Why You Have Lady Problems*

Tormenting Spirits
https://a.co/d/dAogEJf

Triangular Power *(series)*

    Powers Above

SUNBLOCK

Do Not Swear by the Moon

STARSTRUCK

Uncontested Doom

Upgrade: How to Get Out of Survival Mode

Toxic Souls (Book 2 of series)

Legacy (Book 3 of series)

Warfare Prayer Against Beauty Curses

Warfare Prayer Against Poverty

What Have You to Declare?

When the Devourer is Rebuked

The Wilderness Romance *(series)*

- *The Social Wilderness*
- *The Sexual Wilderness*
- *The Spiritual Wilderness*